The King of Cages!

The King of Cages!

✦

How one man used two cages to live a Wildlife Management Dream!

Mark E. Dotson

iUniverse, Inc.
New York Lincoln Shanghai

The King of Cages!
How one man used two cages to live a Wildlife Management Dream!

Copyright © 2007 by Mark E. Dotson

iUniverse books may be ordered through booksellers or by contacting:

iUniverse
2021 Pine Lake Road, Suite 100
Lincoln, NE 68512
www.iuniverse.com
1-800-Authors (1-800-288-4677)

Visit our homepage at http://www.AAllAnimalControl.com

ISBN-13: 978-0-595-42370-5 (pbk)
ISBN-13: 978-0-595-86706-6 (ebk)
ISBN-10: 0-595-42370-1 (pbk)
ISBN-10: 0-595-86706-5 (ebk)

Printed in the United States of America

"To our Lord Jesus Christ for my strength and shield of courage".

To my wife, Alisa, who believes in me. To my daughter, Jessica, who named our business and my daughter, Taylor, whose curiosity is so much fun.

To our franchise owners whose friendship and teamwork keep us going straight up!

A special "Thank You" goes out to Aimee. Without your help, it would have been a long road ahead!

And a big "Thank You" goes out to our suppliers who make the impossible, possible.

Contents

Bio for Mark E. Dotson ix

Foreword. xi

Where it all began 1

Sick and Tired. 6

You Want to do What for a Living!. 8

Hang on to Your Hat!. 12

Smooth and Bumpy Sailing. 16

Growing by Leaps and Bounds 19

Why Not Let Others do What I do? 22

Rolling it Out 25

What Does It Take To Do Well? 31

Where We Are Going 34

It's YOUR Future! 36

Bio for Mark E. Dotson

Mark E. Dotson is the Chief Executive Officer of A All Animal Control, a Nuisance Wildlife Management firm with offices nationwide.

Mark brings twenty years of expertise to the field of Wildlife Management and Animal Damage Control.

Mark is a Certified Wildlife Control Professional, Certified Wildlife Professional, Academy Certified Professional, Certified Bird Control Expert, Certified Geese Management Professional, Certified Marksman and a BCI Certified Bat Removal Specialist.

Mark lives in Charleston, West Virginia, with his wife, Alisa, and stepsons, Trey and Marc. He works out of the corporate location in the city and a satellite office neatly tucked away in the woods. Mark is also the corporate trainer and consultant for A All Animal Control franchises.

Foreword

♦

By Mark E. Dotson

Navigating the business world can be tricky at best. There are many potholes, twists and curves on the road ahead for anyone going it alone.

Owning a business is one of the greatest freedoms we have in the United States. A business allows us to unlock the doors to financial freedom, job security and best of all, have an asset to sell when you want to retire or move on to your next journey in life.

Having been self employed now for many years, there is nothing better in my mind that one can do than own your own business. To be able to control your own destiny and create the life that you have always wanted is a very powerful way to live. You are not simply existing; you are living a life of fulfillment.

I am constantly amazed by the creative people out there that are carving out their own niche in this world and doing things not possible 10 years ago. The advent of the Internet has created many opportunities that simply did not exist before. There is online shopping, online printing, eBay and so many other businesses that are charting and navigating new waters. Some will succeed but many will fail.

Our future as Wildlife Management Professionals appears to be very bright. With the population continuing to grow and more loss of wildlife habitat, our services will be in high demand for years to come! We eagerly await the future!

Where it all began

THE GUIDE — Wednesday, March 6, 1974

' Round The Bend--Hooray!

IN THE SPRING A YOUNG MAN'S FANCY...

In the spring a young man's fancy lightly turns to thoughts of love but a very young man's fancy seriously turns to thoughts of fishing and wiggly worms and wet feet and dogs with waggy tails.

This intrepid half dozen, very young men, were in quest of the finny fishes Saturday afternoon in White Lick Creek which meanders through Arbuckle Acres.

From the left are Roger Duncan, Steve Dotson, Kevin Dotson, Mark Dotson, Ronnie Duncan, and David Fuller. The beagle belongs to the Duncans. His name is Poochie.

I had always enjoyed being outdoors as a kid and never seemed to be indoors for very long. I remember checking some snares one particular winter and the wind chill was 70 below. I bundled up with every bit of winter clothing that I owned and strolled past my father as he was about to head to work. He gave me the look as if I was out of my mind and I was off in the darkness to see if I had caught anything. Seeing was a problem as it was so cold my eye lashes would freeze shut when I closed my eyes! As I approached each snare, I would find nothing in them. It seemed that the foxes were smarter than I and had stayed in their dens!

Growing up in Central Indiana was a child's dream come true. There were so many opportunities to hunt, fish and trap. So many things to explore and you could ride your bike for miles on end and not have a worry in the world.... other than a flat tire.

We didn't worry about crime. It was a place where you could enjoy life and feel safe.

As a young man, I eagerly embraced each of the four seasons. Springtime would bring mushroom hunting and the beginning of the fishing season. I enjoyed watching the newborn wildlife emerge and the trees take on their new foliage. It always seemed like a magical time of year. It was. It was beautiful to watch the landscape slowly transform from the bland colors of winter to bright greens, yellows and purples. Flowers would spring up and trees would start to bud out and new leaves would form. Temperatures would begin to rise and cool, warmer days would begin to take shape, leaving winter behind. Nature would emerge. The snakes would begin to come out; the Robins would arrive and so would the Swallows. You knew that spring was well on its way.

Spring would also bring some very intense storms, including tornadoes. There is nothing like watching a lightning storm from miles away from the comfort of home. The geography was so flat that you could see huge storms rolling in long before they were in your neighborhood. Indiana had some violent weather but it never seemed to last for long. When the weather subsided, I would be off again exploring and finding something to get into.

Summer came on strong and with it came the heat and humidity that would make me want to spend the day at a lazy fishing hole, tucked under a bridge somewhere. I didn't have a lot of opportunity for game fishing, so I would opt to catch big carp (that often snapped my lines) or catfish. I would wait for a large rainfall and then go after the catfish with great ferocity. Using 3 poles at a time, it was not uncommon to have 3 fish on! You stayed busy the whole time you were fishing!

Ahh ... summer. Back then it seemed to last forever. I was out of school for what seemed like an eternity. School was out from at least the middle of May to after Labor Day. That much time allowed me to really pack a lot into the hours of each day and weeks on end. So much to explore, forts to build, fish to be caught, frogs to be chased after and of course.... those dreaded chores. We couldn't escape cutting the grass, pulling weeds, cleaning your room and working in the garden. My father always had a huge garden. With 4 boys in the family, it required a pile of food to feed them all. He always had a great variety of beans, corn, tomatoes and just about everything you could want to eat, fresh from the garden.

The chores didn't last forever and off I went. There were a few neighborhood boys that would gather together and ride bikes all day. We really didn't have any stores near us, so if we wanted a candy bar or drink; it would be many miles to ride to get there. And ride we did!

It was also during the summer that I would work for a local farmer taking care of livestock. He complained one day about the rats that were eating the cracked corn that was used to feed the hogs. I asked him if I could set some traps to catch them and he agreed. It wasn't long and I had the rodent population controlled! This was my first endeavor into the Nuisance Wildlife field.

Autumn is a beautiful time in Indiana. In the area where I grew up, there were only patches of woods. You really didn't get to see the fall foliage in great abundance unless you were in the southern part of the state. But just the same, it was spectacular with the trees that we did have. The first frosts would also hint at hunting season! Squirrels, rabbits and other small game were usually on the hunting menu and we would chase them just about every day. It was quite a challenge carrying a shotgun that was about as big as I was. The weight of the gun and the animals that you bagged were enough to wear you out if you had to travel a long way. Like they say, "If it doesn't kill you, it will make you stronger!"

I didn't hunt with very many people growing up. My brothers did not hunt much, so I would hunt with close friends. Chasing rabbits in big patches of briars sure is easier with someone, especially if you do not have a dog.

I had a Redbone coon hound for a couple years that proved to be a fairly good dog. Coon hunting allowed me to extend my hunting hours of the day too! Coon hunting also was a great teacher and it taught me many things about the feeding habits, habitat and travel patterns of the raccoons.

Whatever it was, I found a way to hunt or trap it. I became proficient in catching muskrats, fox and raccoon. I loved to hunt squirrels back then, as much as I love to today. I don't know what it is about hunting squirrels. Maybe it is the peacefulness of the woods or just the challenge of trying to shoot such a small target that is running high in the trees. Just sitting there with my back to a big oak tree and enjoying the blessing of being in the woods is something that most people never get to experience. What a shame that is. How can people live near the woods and not want to enjoy them? I will never understand it.

I would continue to trap until the final day of the season. Sometimes I would save up all my furs and take them to an auction, but normally I would take them to a local fur buyer. My skills for putting up fur at that time were not good at all. That would come in later years. As a trapper, this is where I learned that wildlife needed management to help control numbers and decrease disease potential by overpopulation. An area can only carry so much population before nature takes its course and wipes them all out. By managing population levels, diseases are kept in check and there is enough food left for the existing populations of wildlife. Being a trapper also taught me how to humanely work with animals. You do not want the animal to unnecessarily feel pain and you want to prevent any pain if possible. Trappers are very skilled at what they do and are very conscientious about how the animal is treated.

Winter was not exactly my most favorite time of year. Sure, I liked to track animals in the snow, but the cold never really was my favorite thing. It seemed to snow quite a bit when I was a boy. We had snow on the ground most of the winter and would break out the sleds. But being in Indiana, there really were not any hills to ride them down. We would have to take our sleds to a local park or other area where we had a hill big enough to make the trip worthwhile.

Snow was a great learning tool. I could look at the fox's tracks in the snow and see how they traveled. I would learn how they walk and what they stopped to check out. This was very valuable information and I would track them for miles wondering where they would den up. I never did find a den, but I sure had a lot of fun trying! It is so neat to see where a fox and a rodent crossed paths. The scene of the chase lay out in front of me and my imagination had to figure it all out.

Winter seemed to last a long time and I was always ready for spring right about the beginning of the year. Once Christmas and New Years were over … it should be spring! Besides, there is not much left that is legal to hunt or trap after February!

Oh well … I was just going to have to wait.

Sick and Tired

It was Monday morning and I was driving to work thinking, "Man, I hate this job." Each and every day was an exercise in the same thing. Get up early in the morning, shower, get dressed, eat breakfast, pack a lunch and fight the Denver traffic to go to work at the sheet metal shop. All that just to go to a job that I hated!

(It hadn't been that long ago that I had finished my service in the Air Force after fighting in a war. I was beginning to think that I would rather go back to the war. At least I didn't hate being there!)

Day after day, I would make that drive to Denver to an assortment of different jobs over the years. All of them either working in an office, warehouse or shop, of sorts. I was an outside person working in an inside world. I couldn't go places and felt chained to the company I worked for, besides living paycheck to paycheck. I was stuck. Stuck in a huge rut and nothing could pull me out.

After you work in a job you don't like for a while, you begin to rationalize why you are working there. You tell yourself things like, "I am doing this to feed my family" or "I am only going to work this job until I find the right job". You become complacent and start to feel comfortable in your job and you stop looking for that right job that you have always wanted to do. You give up and give out. You resign yourself to the fact that this will be what you are going to do for the rest of your life.

And why does it seem like an eternity from the start of your shift until the end of it? You find things to occupy your time and prevent you from losing your mind during your daily routine. But when are you really going to lose your mind? When are you going to say the wrong thing or do the wrong thing that may lead to your termination? Hmm … seems like I did that a couple times! I was beginning to figure out that I was a leader, not a follower.

Daily life at the job begins to wear on you and something has to give. It might be you giving out or getting out! That is when you really start to become unhappy in your life. Statistics say that 85% of the people in the United States hate their job or don't like it in some way. 85%! That is a lot of people. I would equate it to being in a bad marriage and feeling trapped and helpless. Maybe even hopeless.

So, now what was I going to do? That question seemed to keep occurring in my mind and with more unhappiness; it came to mind more often. Why be unhappy when I have a choice to do what I wanted to do in this world? It was time for me to make a change, but how? I had a wife and two young daughters. How would I be able to do what I have always wanted to do and support a family? What if I failed and lost everything? How would I grow the business?

All of these questions were overwhelming at the time but I decided it was time to step out in faith and give it a try. What did I have to lose? I already hated my job and was absolutely miserable there.

You Want to do What for a Living!

I got a call from a neighbor that had squirrels in their attic. I had an old cage lying in the garage. I grabbed it and came over to investigate the problem. I thought that this is just squirrels; it can't be that big of a deal. I removed the squirrels and did a small repair on the home. I was hooked!

I decided to start a part time business and make a go of it.

At first, it was slow going. I took out a small Yellow Page ad and the phone started to ring a little more. Now it was the time to make it or break it. The phone wasn't ringing enough to satisfy me and I wanted to get a larger piece of the Denver market.

I began to study the area and the marketplace. There were plenty of competitors, but I didn't think they were tapping into all of the business. There had to be so much more that could be done and I was determined to go out and find it.

The wildlife was abundant and I could see where homes had wildlife conflicts. Why were those people not calling me? Could they not find me? My ad was in the Yellow Pages. Did they know they had a wildlife problem? They had to! When you have a squirrel in your attic, you almost always know it! What was I doing wrong?

Was I doing anything wrong? Maybe not. I continued to study the Denver market and began to learn about marketing. I thought to myself, "This marketing thing can't be that hard." "What is the mystery behind all of the hype that goes on with marketing?", I said to myself. I didn't think that it was some magical force that only people with advanced degrees could do. They might have a degree, but I have two things they probably don't have: abundant common sense and a determination that nothing will stop me! You can't learn that in any school. The school of hard knocks is a good teacher if you pay attention. If you didn't, you would pay the price!

"Well", I thought to myself, "I can stay in business only as long as I can afford my mistakes." Each area of marketing was looked at and I started writing down different techniques to try. Direct mail, radio, press articles, brochures and any other things that came to mind. I became a full time student in the school of marketing, to say the least. My daughters would spend time stuffing envelopes with me at night and then we would make trips to the Post Office together. They were having as much fun as I was and it was a great way to spend quality time with them! I would crank things out on the old inkjet printer as fast as it could go. I wore out a couple printers and who knows how much I spent on ink cartridges! Before long I became my own printing press. The marketing machine was slowly coming to life and beginning to be fine tuned.

Now what? Little by little the phone started ringing more. I was beginning to get fairly comfortable with doing the work but needed to work on selling the jobs. Sales ... now there is something to learn.

Everybody has their own style of selling. Some are hard sell, others soft sell and still others are in between. Some people find it easy to sell and some don't like the process at all. I guess I was in the middle somewhere. I like the interaction with the client, but was not one to "push anything down someone's throat". I had been in many sales situations and detested someone trying to hard sell me. I can make up my own mind and decide whether I want something or not! I thought that most people were of the same mindset. They would do their research and make an informed decision. Hard selling is old school. People these days want choices and someone trying to sell them the old way just simply doesn't work.

People want value for their dollar and a lot of benefits to the service they are hiring. Some want the lowest cost product or service and either can't afford quality or don't understand quality. Quality comes at a price. Rolex, BMW, Cadillac, Lear Jet and DeBeers are all brands that come to mind when I think of quality. Sometimes convincing people to pay more for a product or service that will save them a lot of money in the long run is a difficult task. And, you may never succeed if they are set on only buying based on the price.

I needed to attract clients that understood quality and send those that didn't to the cheap guys in town. The cheap guys didn't care about service and how their company was reflected in the market. My thought was if we provided a service for a cheap price, it was perceived as a cheap value. In other words, you get what you pay for. There are no truer words in the universe.

Now that I had this marketing thing and sales thing to figure out, my vision was becoming clearer about what the future of this business should look like.

It was time to start organizing this business.

My first Service Truck

Hang on to Your Hat!

When I started ramping up the business, a need for procedures, methods and techniques had to be implemented. There were start up procedures, marketing, sales and safety procedures, wildlife control methods and techniques and so much more.

I got a legal pad and began writing down all of these procedures. I had to have a structure to this business and not rely on my memory to run it. How could I let other employees do their jobs without a set of procedures to do it? The simple answer is that I could not.

As I started writing all of the things I had to do on a day to day basis, I began to realize that there are a whole lot of hats to wear when you run your own business! I was wearing the personnel hat, the accounting hat, employee, employer and many others. I was switching hats at an ever increasing pace as the business grew. Now, how do I make sense of all this hat switching business? I was soon going to find out!

As life has a way of throwing curves at me, in the winter of 1997, my wife left and took our two daughters to Florida. As you can imagine, my life was turned upside down. The most precious thing to me in the world had been taken away from me and I was going to fight to get my children back.

About this time, I was out working on a client's home and while I was up on a ladder, we began talking. Out of the clear blue, he asked me if there was something wrong. I began to hem and haw and finally said, "Yes, there is something that has been bothering me." I came down off the ladder and told him the story about the wife and kids. He invited me into his home and said he had something for me. He retreated to a back room and came back carrying a small book. He asked me if we could pray together and I was hesitant, but said yes. He prayed about my situation and asked God to come into my life and provide comfort and peace. He asked me if I would like to invite Jesus into my heart. I said yes and as I prayed for that, it felt like the weight of the world had come off my shoulders. I was no longer carrying around this huge burden with me. God had just taken it from me. I cannot describe how good I finally felt after all of that heartache. To this day, I still don't remember what that small book was that he gave me, but it really didn't matter. I had something inside of me that was real and I had given my heart to Jesus.

I walked out of that house, said goodbye and drove down the road with a feeling of total empowerment. I was no longer powerless. I never did see that man again, but I had finally begun to live life.

I started to dig in deeper and grow the business. Along came a wonderful lady named Aimee looking for a job as a technician. I interviewed her and immediately hired her! She was full of energy and was very sharp. I knew I had a winner on board. We split up Denver into two areas and began to work those hard. Anything outside the area would usually go to me and I would travel to whatever projects needed accomplished.

Before long, it was time to hire another technician to replace me in the field because the office work was becoming more than I could handle with the field work. The ads were placed in the local paper looking for a technician. There were a lot of applicants, but not many that were qualified to do the type of work we do. To find someone that I could instantly put to work and be productive was next to impossible.

A training program was in need of being implemented. But first, I wanted to separate the wheat from the chaff. Before I was going to hire someone that might not work out, I began to take applicants on a ride along for a day to observe them and how they performed in the field. If they showed a fear of heights or if they just sat in the truck when we pulled up to the client's house, they were immediately dropped from my list of candidates.

In the summer of 1999, I suddenly found myself raising my two daughters by myself after my divorce. The business had now grown to 4 employees. I had to figure out a way to stay completely in the office and take care of my children. They were very young then and needed their dad and his time.

Now I realized that I had to completely replace myself in all areas of the business. Great.... how was I going to do that?

Bookkeeping was never a part of the business that I really enjoyed doing. This was the first place that I started replacing myself. I interviewed several people and found someone that was a very hard worker and detail oriented. Her name was Christy and she stayed with us for the next 6 years as our full time accounting support. Christy owned her own business and we simply outsourced this part of the business to her. With that off my shoulders, I looked around and decided it was time to get my office in order. I was a very organized person, but my office needed the tools to become organized as well. I hired an organizational consultant to come in and completely turn my office upside down and then make it right again. She did an incredible job and built a great foundation for our office systems. So, the bookkeeping was set up and the office organized, now I could really get to work!

I started working on the business but not in the business. Aimee and I were trading off the phones. I was taking them in the morning and she was answering them in the afternoon. That was working out great and allowed us to schedule our technicians and handle the administrative functions that came along with a 4 truck operation. There were still times I had to go out in the field to meet clients and do an emergency job. For the most part I was in the office and could finally be the visionary that the company needed me to be.

Smooth and Bumpy Sailing

Like all things in life, there is going to be some smooth sailing and just some bumps that really catch you off guard. The business was going along well and things were growing at a very fast pace. We had a decent crew of technicians and then all of a sudden two of them quit! I thought to myself, great ... now I have to jump back out in the field again, hire replacements, train them and then I will be able to work in the office again. This was one of the hardest times in the business. Things are fine and clicking along when I had a full crew and everyone was doing their job. But when someone up and quits, things got a bit chaotic.

I went back to my notepad and started to write more procedures and implement them. It was time to take a more serious approach to my business and start to be stricter in the policies I set out. I never liked to baby sit someone. My employees would receive their assignments and were expected to get the job done. Most of the time this would work out fine, but with some employees, they constantly needed someone holding their hand. These people soon found the exit door as they just didn't make an overall contribution to my team. I needed people with a great deal of common sense, some wildlife knowledge and a general knowledge of home repairs. I wasn't looking for rocket scientists!

One day I was sitting in my office and I heard someone come to the door. It was an agent from the Colorado Department of Agriculture. I invited the gentleman in and he began asking questions about what we did and if we used any chemicals, etc. I explained our operation to him in detail. At the end of our discussion, he gave me a cease and desist order and demanded that I shut down my business! I asked him why and he stated, "Because there is wording in the regulations that if you use a trap, you must have a pest control license". I about went through the roof at this point and said that is insane. We don't use any chemicals, why should we have a pest control license? He didn't have much of an answer to that. I suspected all along that someone had called the Department of Agriculture and "turned us in". This was not the first time that one of my competitors would try and put me out of business. I was not breaking any laws. What I did next really blew their minds. Within a few hours, I hired a qualified supervisor with a pest control license. I got in touch with the Colorado Department of Agriculture and got a pest control license for my company. They had never seen anything like this before and couldn't believe it. I was not going to let anyone take my company down!

Well, to say the least, that competitor trying to defeat me just empowered me even more! The Bible says for those who believe "no weapon that is formed against thee shall prosper". I truly believe that.

At first, what I thought was a very bad thing happening to my business turned out to be a very good thing! Some of the best things that have happened to me in my life have come from the very worst things.

With new doors being opened with a new employee, I could have him do things like treat for mice and rats and work on our pigeon control programs.

I started watching our competition and noticed that a lot of what they were doing was copying what I was doing! At first, I was mad that they couldn't come up with their own ideas. But then I knew I had them all on the run. They were copying me because they could not beat me and some of them had been around a lot longer than I had been. So, I had to be a step ahead of them all the time. It served to keep me sharp and to define how I would operate on a national basis.

Imagine this ... I was the little guy who just started out with two traps, an old truck and now I was hitting the oldest companies around in the shins. It felt pretty good knowing that I could compete with them.

Now that I had them scrambling, now what? Dig in deeper!

Again, out came the notebook and by now, I had a binder full of information that was about an inch thick. I was starting to really get somewhere. God was blessing me very well.

It was time to strengthen the areas of my business that needed it and grow it out some more.

Growing by Leaps and Bounds

The business was taking on a life of its own. The phones would ring nonstop from Monday through Friday and regularly on the weekend. Business was booming! Then it happened. A major phone line was cut in our area and it took out all our lines! This spelled major disaster if we couldn't get this fixed quickly.

A couple days went by and I was calling in with my cell phone to the main voice mail to check messages about every 15 minutes. I had about enough and thought there had to be something that could be done about this. I called the phone company and they said they could do an emergency transfer of all calls to my cell phone. I said "Hoorah!". This was the answer I needed. We started to catch up with all of the calls and work that was coming in but I still don't know how much work was lost with the downed lines. It was more than a week later that the phone company had the lines restored. What a mess.

But I learned something from that mess. I had to have a back up plan or a contingency plan for when things do go wrong. And believe me, things will go wrong.

Once the phones and fax lines and Internet (back then there was not any DSL, so I was using dial up), were up and running, things got back to normal. Now I could go back to working on the business again.

It was time to expand my territory. I already worked most of the Denver metro area, but it was time to branch out to areas beyond Denver. I marketed to the Loveland/Fort Collins areas and began to slowly service these areas. The territories of my employees were enlarged and I brought on a carpenter to help with repair work. We became a full service Wildlife Management company and could resolve the problem and repair just about anything that needed it. My little business was growing up. It was beginning to become a mature business is some ways, but still had a ways to go.

Service was a very important part of who I was and when I told someone I was going to do something, I did it. There was no "I might be there". I honored my word and I wanted to instill that in everyone that worked for me. Service was not just a 7 letter word, it was something that we wanted to live and breathe. I wanted to provide incredible service and take extraordinary care of our clients. If a complaint came into the office, I would see to it personally and if we were wrong, I would make it right. There was never a question about making it right for our clients. I gave my employees the power to make it right and not have to ask permission from me.

As you can see, I was climbing the ladder of success! All 40 feet of it!

I started to get quite popular with some of the media and began to get a reputation as a company that cared about its people, the wildlife and the community. We are given a big responsibility when we become wildlife managers and that responsibility was not taken lightly by me. I frequently was interviewed on television or radio and had articles written about my company.

I was now in the spotlight and in some sense, I was a pioneer. But the pioneers were the ones who took the arrows too. Luckily, I didn't get many arrows in me! I ran my business correctly and did the right thing even if it felt wrong. I guaranteed our work, took great care of my clients and worked long hours to make sure we did the best we could. Sure, there were some people we could never please, but you will find those in every business!

Mark Dotson hangs colored streamers on a house to deter woodpeckers, which have pecked holes in the stucco. Dotson and other pest-control specialists are busy this time of year evicting urban wildlife.

Animal evictions
Pesky houseguests often arrive in spring; trapper ushers them out

My other office.... on the ladder.

Why Not Let Others do
What I do?

The thought finally dawned on me that I could be helping other people do what I love so much to do. This was the most incredible business in the world and why don't I share that with other people? How? I could train people and open offices in different states, but that sounded like a lot to manage. I had heard of franchising, but really didn't know much about it. I decided to go talk to a franchise attorney and see what all that entailed. I met with the attorney and saw that this was the way we wanted to go.

Armed with this knowledge, I strengthened my operations manual, put together the rest of the franchise package and paperwork and started advertising for franchisees. It was the year 2000 and I had been advertising for about 3 months and the first candidate came to me. After working with the candidate for a couple months, he called one day and said he had lost his job and would like to join our team. Wow! My first franchise owner! In a month, I had him down to my office for training and then sent him back to Omaha to open our first location outside of Colorado. I was thrilled.

Those first franchise results astounded me. I couldn't believe how well he did. He took my system, implemented it and really blew us away. Things were good and I continued to coach and support his office and watched him grow.

My Denver office was still growing but was leveling off a bit now. I had to keep that business going and provide for ways to grow our new franchise. It was a balancing act, but helping one helped the other. More marketing, sales and field procedures were developed. My Internet site was modified to include more information about the company and to promote our franchise office.

Leads slowly were coming into our office for new franchisees. I wanted the best people to reflect our business and was very particular about who I let operate a franchise. They would be representing A All Animal Control and had to be top notch. We are a faith based organization and the individual has to reflect the values that the Bible teaches. In the business world today, those values are often forgotten and fly by night companies have sprung up everywhere. I just don't understand the mentality of people who start a company and try to rip people off. It always turns out the same for them and their company and even the biggest of companies take the fall for it. If you do business the right way, it will be blessed.

Things were clipping along well … and then it happened.

9-11-2001

A day in infamy. Karen, our data entry person, was in my office at the computer and I had stepped out to check the morning news. I turned on the TV and noticed the World Trade Center was on fire. I figured it must be a movie of some kind, so I surfed onto the next channel and the same image was playing. I knew then that what I was viewing was real. I yelled at Karen to come and check it out. We both sat there for what seemed hours watching this awful event unfold in front of our eyes.

Our phones were silent that day. We might have had 3 calls all day and our usual volume was about 75 to 100. I knew that we were going to be in serious trouble if the phone didn't start ringing again. I had a marketing program scheduled to be rolled out that week, but called and asked them to hold it for a week.

I immediately launched a condolence message on the website, put American flags on our trucks and sent letters to all of our current clients expressing our sadness for the events that unfolded. Having a contingency plan in place helped, but nothing prepares you for something like this. We would be goners if something didn't happen soon and the phones start ringing again.

Within a week they did. Not to the normal call volume, but they were ringing and we continued to expand our marketing into other nontraditional ways. I knew we were in for a heck of a ride, so we tightened our belt and held on for dear life. It would be months before things got back to normal and I could breathe a sigh of relief.

I had to seriously look at my options about laying off people and cutting back on expenses. I was fortunate that I didn't have to lay anyone off. Expenses were cut back, but nothing that hurt us in any way.

Rolling it Out

It was October, after 9-11-01, that I received a call to tell me that my grandfather had passed away. This was another big blow at a time that I was struggling to get the business going full steam again.

I made the trip back east to attend his funeral and I came back to my family's home afterwards to spend time with them. It was warm and beautiful in the hills of Nicholas County, West Virginia. I spent some time in the woods on my grandparent's property as I didn't normally get to see the trees like this. There are not many trees on the plains of the Front Range in Colorado. I was soaking it all in and enjoying this beautiful place.

During this time, I was feeling an urge to move back to West Virginia to be near my family. Something inside me told me to sell the Denver office and my home and move there. Sell everything and move! I thought about it for a while but didn't fight it. After I returned to Denver, unexpectedly, a couple approached me about purchasing the business. My house went on the market. I had one offer and they bought it. It all came together so well that I knew I didn't design the move. A Higher Power was moving me.

My daughters and I packed up a huge rental truck, hooked up a trailer with my truck on it and we were off to live in a home we had neither visited nor seen before, other than in pictures.

We took a long journey across the country and actually had a great time. I didn't have a business to run other than the franchise corporation and it was nice to take some time off and enjoy this trip. It was

February and the weather was cold but not too bad and there was little snow.

After we had everything moved in and were settled in West Virginia, I thought I would take some time off to do some things. I made some side trips here and there, but the calling to get back to work was as strong as ever. I dug right in and got busy writing manuals, advertising and interviewing potential franchise owners. Our next office was soon to roll out and it would be in Akron, Ohio.

From that point on, I started slowly and consistently opening more offices. I kept searching for the best people in good markets. But I still wanted to offer this opportunity to people from all walks of life and at different economic levels. Sure, it would be easy to own a franchise if you have a lot of money, but what if you didn't? Or, what if you had an existing business that wasn't thriving the way you wanted it to? These were all areas that concerned me and I wanted to broaden the offering to as many qualified people as possible.

To broaden the opportunity, I developed 4 franchise levels to make it easier to join our team. These 4 levels consisted of a micro office for the rural areas, a part-time office, a full time office and an existing business conversion program. This would allow me to be flexible and match the opportunity and territory with the individual to meet their goals and needs. Sometimes a person just wants to do Nuisance Wildlife work part time because they have a great job and an area that will not support a full time office. I saw the need to offer these different levels and this really gave a boost to the people who did not have the funds to go all out with a full time business.

I was a firm believer that it doesn't take money to make money. It takes smart thinking to make money. It takes a great system to make money. Sure money helps, but you could have all the money in the world, but without motivation or belief in yourself, your business is not going to prosper.

By creating the different levels, I could now grow the business in areas I could not before.

I started having people from all walks of life contact me. I already had franchise owners that came from a variety of backgrounds. I had an IBM computer engineer, a pharmaceutical salesman, painting contractors, a truck driver and a factory worker. I really found out that just about anyone could do well in this type of business if they could do 3 things:

1.   Make a decision to change their life

2.   Commit to that decision

3.   Resolve to learn how to do what I do

That was really it. Those 3 simple things and I could take a person and train, coach and support them until they had their own little, thriving business and were confident in doing business. Once that happened, people's lives were changed forever. They enjoyed what they were doing and poured their hearts into it. My satisfaction came from the fact that they could take my system, implement it step by step and run their own business whether it is in Denver, Colorado or Roanoke, Virginia. It didn't matter where they were, they would follow the system and it would prosper.

On the next pages are a few of my franchise owners "who make it all happen".

Without team members like these, I would not be where I am today.

Tim Stevens, Roanoke, VA

Jack Thompson, Puget Sound, WA

Russell Staley, Tulsa, OK

Joshua Jones, Tri-State MO

Kelly Stiefermann, Central MO

What Does It Take To Do Well?

It takes faith and a belief in yourself more than anything. If you know you are going to fail, you will fail. If you know that you are going to succeed, you will succeed. It is an attitude that you will make it in whatever field you have chosen in life.

In business, it takes a great system, hard work and smart work to do well. Nothing in life that is great comes with ease. If it does, then it usually is not worthwhile or lasting. It is like someone giving you something. It might seem great at the time, but it is more valuable to you if you had to work for it and earn it.

The most successful people in the world generally have worked hard for what they have. Sure, some of them inherited what they have and didn't work a day in their lives, but most worked at their career and made good choices.

If you are going to succeed at anything in life, you must not give it a half hearted attempt. Either you give it your all or just don't even try. What would be the point?

Yes, you might try something and it not succeed. I had a small mail order business before I opened my Nuisance Wildlife Business and it was an absolute failure! I gave it my all but it didn't survive. I really wasn't prepared for that business and was winging it in an area I knew little about. But that lesson taught me a tremendous amount. If Thomas Edison quit after 9,999 times of trying to make the light bulb, we wouldn't have the light bulb! It took him 10,000 times to get it right! The real failure is failing to try.

First and foremost you must have faith. Faith in God and faith in yourself. If God is calling you to open your own business, He will either empower you or equip you to do it. If God calls you to do something, He will not call you to fail. If God wants you to do anything in life, He will open the door for you. Are the doors in your life being opened?

My moving to West Virginia wasn't by chance but was a result of God opening all the doors for me. I didn't have to lift a finger to make any of it happen. It just happened like it was magic ... or divine intervention.

Patience and persistence are two other characteristics that one must have. Nothing comes quickly in this world and there are no get rich schemes. People who get rich slowly and methodically are the ones who create and keep the true wealth they earn. They may not have the most exciting life in the world, but they have the money to do whatever their heart desires.

Persistence is what keeps you going through the thick and thin. I have had plenty of both and without persistence; I would have never made it.

What has made me successful is taking great care of our people and letting them be accountable for their success. I give them the tools and system to succeed.

One other thing I wanted to mention to people who are married and considering starting their own business. Ask your spouse if he or she will totally support you in this decision. Without your spouse believing and supporting you in this decision, they will inevitably hold you down or possibly cause your business to fail. It is vital to have the support from your wife or husband in anything you do. If you don't, that is a major red flag and you may want to avoid attempting it.

Where We Are Going

Our industry is poised for consistent growth for many years to come. Technology will change and our methods will be redefined, but our core processes will remain the same. People will always have wildlife conflicts and they will need someone to resolve them. As less and less people have interactions with wildlife, it will create an atmosphere of fear and uncertainty about how to deal with a wildlife problem.

Sure, they can Google for answers, but Google isn't going to come out and remove the raccoons from their chimney!

A All Animal Control will continue to develop as a national company and fill the niche for resolving wildlife problems. Our core business will remain the same and we will continue to meet a need in the marketplace with the expertise of our many qualified team members.

We plan to grow the company to all 50 states and internationally. There are many opportunities around the globe that we will eventually tap into and create a very strong brand in every market that we serve.

We will continue to innovate and create new technologies, techniques and procedures to keep up with our changing world. We want to be the pioneers of this industry and be good stewards of what we have been blessed with. The generations of our owners depend on me to keep focused on ways to make their offices better equipped, trained and ready to capitalize on their markets.

Being good conservationists is an important principle that we want to leave as our legacy in this world. By doing the right things with the way we manage our wildlife problems, we can protect the wildlife at the same time we are removing them. Our techniques will continue to be perfected and allow us more flexibility in our control methods.

With new technology constantly emerging, the future is very exciting in the field of Wildlife Management!

It's YOUR Future!

If you have seriously considered working in the area of Wildlife Management, these are some tips that will help you get on the right track to success.

Wildlife work requires a special person who is not afraid "to go where the wildlife goes". Our work finds us in attics, crawlspaces and on roofs. It takes a person who can think on their feet and have a bit of a creative side or just a lot of good, old, common sense. You have to be part investigator, part animal controller and part client service representative. It takes someone who has a desire to learn, who possesses discipline, integrity, honesty, some knowledge of wildlife and a general knowledge and the skills to do small home repairs.

Also, if you are considering this type of work, some preparation is in order. First, it would be good to have an educational background in Wildlife Biology or Biology in general. Wildlife damage management course work would be preferred and as much hands-on or internship programs as possible will help make you an instantly valuable member of any team.

Employers are looking for people who can communicate, are organized and who work well with the general public. Self-confidence is a must, as this translates into your clients trusting you to be their Wildlife Expert! But most of all, a professional attitude and demeanor is very important, as you will be working with live animals and the publics' perception of how you deal with them is very important.

Working with wildlife is fascinating. There are so many different things that you can do in this field and new opportunities will open up all the time. There are people doing endangered species surveys, removing invasive species, monitoring movements with GPS units and so much more. Even the tiniest of creatures are being studied and monitored. It is a rapidly changing world and with that change comes more pollution, less habitat for wildlife and more challenges to meet. Hopefully as man gains more knowledge, he will be able to overcome things like pollution, toxic chemicals, structures that injure and kill wildlife and ones that prevent wildlife from free roaming and interfere with migratory routes.

Wildlife is on this planet for all of us to enjoy. Some simply love to view and photograph while others enjoy hunting and fishing. As long as there is balance in what we do, we will all be able to enjoy it. And if we do it responsibly, our wildlife will be around for generations to come. We need to keep the air, soil and water clean because our wildlife is usually the first indicator of a toxic environment. The fish start to disappear from the streams and eventually even the larger game is affected.

With our world becoming more global, our country is becoming a haven for invasive species. Zebra mussels, Nutria and Brown Tree Snakes are just a few of the many species we are fighting right now. As more and more cargo pours into this country through our ports, more exotic species will come along with that cargo. The challenge to keep these invasive species out of the country will be harder than ever. Once they move into our sometimes predator free world, they can multiply and take over whole ecosystems like the rabbits that were imported into Australia.

With so many opportunities staring at you today, the world is your oyster. More opportunities will only continue to open up and the future will continue to be bright. One hundred years ago, there was not a lot of work in the wildlife field. You would have been lucky to get a job as a hunting or fishing guide and make any money doing it. Now, you can do both of those or simply guide people on nature walks and interpretive trails and get paid well for it! The world, it is a changing place. Change is good and you must embrace that change and change along with it to thrive and prosper.

In order to succeed in the business world you must educate yourself in as many areas as possible. Have a thirst for knowledge and a passion for what you do. Passion is one of the key things to have in your life that will make you excel above all others. Have passion in everything that you do. Have passion in your relationships with others and just don't simply be there. Think of a person that you know who lives their life with passion. Then think of a person you know who sits in front of the TV from the time they get home until they go to bed…. and sometimes when they get in bed with the TV in the bedroom. Who has the passion in their life, the person in front of the TV or the other person you were thinking of? I bet you know the answer.

You only have one life to live on this earth and you have the power to make it a good one or a bad one. When you make good choices, you have a good life. When you make bad choices, you normally have a bad life. Life is about choices. Thankfully, we live in a country that allows us to be free and make choices. We are free to choose what we want to do as a career, free to drive our car down the road and cross into another state without any papers and free to be who we want to be. With those freedoms comes a responsibility to be the best you can be. You are responsible to yourself, your family and for those around you. When you are driving that car, yes, you are responsible for those around you that you don't crash into them.

I have traveled to many areas of the world and I can tell you that there is no other place that I would rather be than in America. We might have our problems, but we are living in the best country in the world, by far. There is no other country where people have the opportunities that we do. Why do you think that people who come to this country (the ones that want to work anyway) have such success? They see the opportunities where you and I may not. When they are on the outside looking in, they have a different perspective and will seize opportunities that may not be obvious to us. We are very blessed with all that we have in America. This country has been good to me and I will continue to give back as much as I can.

With such a bright future, go out and grab hold of your dreams. Find what it is that your heart desires and go for it. Don't be afraid to do something you have not done before and never be afraid to ask. You can have anything in this world that you want if you ask. You just have to ask the right person! Asking someone for a million dollars who only makes twenty thousand a year isn't asking the right person.

You would be amazed at how many doors will come swinging open for you if you simply ask. I have been in so many places simply because I asked. I used to be afraid to ask. I am not afraid anymore and never will be.

Remember, live your life with passion. Be patient and persistent. Success doesn't come overnight like it does on TV. It takes working smart and working hard. Today you have an opportunity like never before to make your life what you want it to be. Years ago you had limits on what you could do. In my part of the country, West Virginia, there were two options, the coal mines or the coal mines. That was life. That was what you did and there were few options outside the coal camps for work. I think you have a few more options today. Go out and take advantage of your options.

Think about these questions and answer them for yourself;

What are your options?

_____

What do you want to do with your life?

_____

What is stopping you from living your dream?

_____

How will you overcome what is stopping you?

_____

A final word.

Working in the Nuisance Wildlife Management field has been the most rewarding and fulfilling thing I have ever done. When I am able to make a difference in my client's lives and improve their quality of life, they are happy beyond compare. And I get paid to do what I love to do! It doesn't get any better than that for me.

I hope that you will investigate the opportunities in the field of Nuisance Wildlife Management and find the right fit for you. Once you envision your dream about what you want to do with your life, then you will be propelled toward it.

A All Animal Control would like to help you make that dream come true. Visit our website at www.aallanimalcontrol.com to learn more about living your dream and working with wildlife.

978-0-595-42370-5
0-595-42370-1